The
Brain Tumours
Wife

By

Carol Shaw

Written and published by Carol Shaw 2017

www.thebraintumourswife.com

Printed by Biddles 2017

Biddles

Castle House,

East Winch Rd,

Blackborough End,

Kings Lynn,

Norfolk

PE32 1SFX

ISBN 978-1-999866099

Typeset in Calibri 12pt by re:creates

Cover photography and design by re:creates

This book is dedicated to my one and only true love,

Robert Shaw,

a true Brain Tumour Warrior.

Love you millions.

"For I know the plans I have for you," declares the LORD,

"plans to prosper you and not to harm you,

plans to give you hope and a future".

Jeremiah 29:11

Contents

Introduction

I suppose I had better start by introducing myself. I am Carol Shaw,

I was born in Worcestershire, but have lived in a number of different places in England whist growing up. I have a sister called Linda, and my parents are still going strong, having just turned eighty years of age. My first marriage ended after 13 years and having spent five years searching for 'Mr Right', I finally found him in 2002. I have now been married to Robert for sixteen years. Robert has a son, Matthew from a previous marriage who is engaged to the lovely Dannika and together they have a delightful little girl, Everley.

I have always worked right from the age of fifteen, when I left school and got a job in a local titanium stockholders business as an office junior. With several promotions and a job change, I climbed the ladder to the point where I found myself working at an International Pharmaceutical Company as the I.T. & Systems Manager. I loved this job and the company was great to work for, but unfortunately there was a merger and I was one of the many who were made redundant.

Luckily, I got a replacement job straight away and worked as an I.T. Consultant, but I didn't really like the constant travelling and being sent all over the U.K. to sort out various I.T. problems. So, when the company was sold and I was made redundant, it was quite a relief, although a shock at the time.

At that time, I had recently met Robert and we had started dating. We met at church, which I guess is quite unusual, via a mutual friend who put us in touch with each other. Robert needed some techy support and as I worked in I.T., I was able to offer him some training to get him up to speed with his new technology. Well, that's what was supposed to happen. Instead we hit it off immediately, and the idea of I.T. training soon went out of the window and forgot about the technology and went on a date instead.

When I was made redundant and found myself looking for a new job, Robert immediately offered me a job in his business, albeit a temporary arrangement until I found something more suitable. I knew he was a keeper, when he phoned me to say he'd bought me a car to replace the company car I had to hand back. I was totally overwhelmed by his generosity, and still am when I see what he does for others without even giving it a second thought.

That was the beginning of our 'happy ever after'. Something we had both dreamed of, having experienced a failed marriage each before. I had been single for five years and was beginning to give up hope of finding 'Mr Right', but kept praying that he would turn up sooner rather than later.

Robert and I married in July 2003 and, as all couples do, we have had our ups and downs. The hardest time was during the recession of 2008 which hit us very hard. We were both self-employed as mortgage brokers and the market literally collapsed overnight. Banks were closing their doors to lending, Northern Rock Building Society practically went out of business. Houses were being repossessed and almost all of our business friends and colleagues were losing their jobs. It was truly horrendous.

I can clearly remember being on holiday in our then holiday home in Spain. It was September 2008, and we woke up to our phones pinging with texts, emails and messages from our friends and colleagues in the UK. Something big was happening. We switched on the news, and to our horror, we watched almost in a daze as the U.K. economy collapsed.

Our holiday was only for a week, but we were dreading coming home to the aftermath. Our fears were nothing compared to what we came home to. From being a successful business arranging around 60+mortgages per month, and earning a good living from it, we went to a big fat zero.

Clients were still coming in asking for mortgages, but the lenders who were still trading at the time stepped up the criteria which made it virtually impossible to meet their new conditions, so our business was at a standstill.

There were also other difficulties as the business was owned by Robert and his then business partner. The business partner, who will remain unnamed, did not conduct his business in a way that sat well with us and it quickly became very evident that we could no longer work with him. We had no option but to walk away from this business with absolutely nothing aside from the knowledge that everything we did, we did with a clear conscience and in an honest and trustworthy manner.

A new business opportunity presented itself, and this was a Godsend and served us well for a season. The mortgage market has never recovered to the extent that it was before the recession and we knew that we had to find an alternative way of earning a living.

Although it was an extremely difficult time, we remained strong in our faith. Even when we knew we had to make the almost impossible decision to let go of our dream home in the country, we knew that God would look after us and point us in the right direction, albeit a different direction to the one we had our eyes focussed upon.

We relocated our home and business back into suburbia; it was a massive change for us as we had everything planned out. We had bought our lovely bungalow with the view to living there until the end of our days. It was now time to jettison everything except the absolute essentials. We had to concentrate on re-building our business and it wasn't too long before we started to get a glimpse of the new business areas we were to become involved in. We used our experiences in the recession to create Debt Relief Solutions (CIC) Ltd, so that we could help people in financial difficulties by educating them to deal with their debts head on. An opportunity was also presented to Robert to transfer his skills to the world of Wills, Probate, Lasting Powers of Attorneys and other legal services, and this has now become his particular area of expertise.

So here we are today and, I remain self employed as a debt and money advisor and money coach via my community interest company, Debt Relief Solutions, which is a not for profit organisation. I also design and make jewellery under the business name Highly Strung. Both businesses are poles apart but I enjoy them equally and am as passionate about helping people in debt as I am sitting designing new masterpieces.

Robert also remains self-employed and has worked in the financial services industry for over 35 years, seeing through many changes, especially in recent years. He has diversified by way of introducing Wills, Property Trusts, Powers of Attorney, Probate and more recently end of life financial planning.

We were doing relatively OK, that is until March 2014, and then our world fell apart....

'The Lord's loving kindnesses indeed never cease,

for His compassions never fail.

They are new every morning;

Great is Your faithfulness'.

Lamentations 3:22-23

The Day It All Changed

Robert had been feeling a bit odd for a few months and had been suffering from dizziness and balance issues for a while too. His hearing loss became evident as we noticed that the volume levels on the television were creeping up slowly. He had also mentioned a strange noise in his head, which we later discovered was tinnitus.

A visit to the G.P. resulted in Robert being referred to the hearing clinic at Heartlands Hospital. Several weeks later at the clinic, they performed a full hearing test and there was no evident cause of the dizziness or vertigo. However, it was standard procedure for anyone suffering from one-sided tinnitus that an M.R.I. scan would be performed just in case.

We can clearly remember the day of the scan, as it was ridiculously early in the morning, about 7.30am I seem to remember. The hospital staff were very busy and when Robert's time came, he was greeted with an abrupt nurse who instructed him to get himself up on the bed whilst they clamped his head in place.

For those of you who have had an M.R.I. scan you will know how difficult it is to keep perfectly still during the procedure. It's almost like your body is trying to do the complete opposite. Fortunately, Robert was able to keep his head still and therefore avoided having to have the scan repeated, and also avoided the wrath of the nurse on duty!

After the scan had been completed, the same nurse came through to help him off the bed, and it was then, that Robert knew something was wrong. The nurse's attitude had changed completely, and was now much more compassionate and she even wished him well as we left the department. Maybe we had imagined it, and she was just having a bad day and had just settled into her early start.

Of course, we looked on the internet to try and second guess what it could be. We looked at Ménière's disease, which is a condition that affects the inner ear due to the build-up of fluid which can in turn affect balance and hearing. So that's it, we thought, it's got to be Ménière's Disease.

We did carry on looking and came across several other conditions it could be, but as you can imagine, Robert's symptoms related to a range of conditions, so we stopped looking on Google after a while.

After a couple of weeks, when Robert arrived back from a routine G.P. appointment one Friday afternoon, he had just gotten through the front door when the phone started ringing. It was Dr Sanghera, the head G.P. from our local practice. He wanted us to come straight back to the surgery to see him, and no, we didn't need an appointment, just get in the car and come straight over. Oh yes, and "would you drive, Mrs Shaw ?". We knew something was obviously wrong, as you can't get appointment at our surgery for gold dust, let alone be called in for one. I cannot imagine what was going through Robert's mind as I drove like a maniac to the surgery, but I knew he was thinking the worst, as was I.

We raced into the surgery and were told we were expected and to go straight in to see Dr Sanghera. He didn't beat about the bush, we sat down, and we said he's received the scan results back and needed to see us straight away.

They had found a brain tumour.

As soon as I heard these words, my mind flew away in a million different directions, So many questions, so many thoughts. My emotions welled up inside me, but I quickly sent them back down again. Bursting into tears at this point would serve no purpose. I remember grabbing Robert's hand, he was as white as a sheet. He sat motionless, staring at the computer screen. Dr Sanghera was talking but neither of us was really listening. It was like we were there in the room, but watching some sort of weird movie playing out before us.

Suddenly, I was back in the room, my mind was now focussed and now I needed to ask questions.

"So, what happens now?", I asked our doctor. He explained that we would be fast tracked to a neurologist to discuss treatment options etc. He also said that he had absolutely no experience with brain tumours so could offer little advice. I looked again at his screen, and at the bottom of the report in big red letters were the words URGENT REFERRAL. Those words made me shudder.

We left the surgery, feeling numb and helpless. I had noted the name of the tumour as an Acoustic Neuroma. I had heard this name before, possibly from our internet browsing, and was eager to learn more. The ten-minute drive home took an eternity, and Robert hardly spoke.

We got home, and then I don't know if it was adrenaline, or just sheer panic, but I texted Matthew to ask him to call me urgently, phoned my parents and told them the news, and then spoke to Robert's brother in law to ask him to break the news to Robert's elderly mother.

Before I go on, I must explain that Robert and I are both Christians. I was brought up in the Church from a little girl as my dad was a minister and I was born again at a very young age. My walk with Christ hasn't always been a straight one, and I strayed from the path as a young adult but had recently come back on track some years before I met Robert. I guess I know that God has always had His hand on my life, even when I ignored Him. My parents have prayed for me my whole life, and I am extremely grateful for their perseverance even when I haven't deserved it. Robert was a new Christian and had a wonderfully innocent and pure faith. He sees God in black and white, He either is the centre of your world or He isn't, you are either a follower or you are not. It's as simple as that in his eyes.

So, it follows, that we telephoned the church, and told them of Robert's diagnosis. Our church is great when people are ill, as they immediately instigate a prayer chain, which reaches across the Midlands and beyond, with everyone praying for you at the time you most need it. The rest of that evening was a blur, I can't remember how we spent it, but that night, we held each other tightly, frightened not to let go, frightened about what would happen next, but secure in the knowledge that our God would look after us no matter what is to follow. It was a very long night, with some tears, lots of hugs, and a massive dose of prayer.

The next morning, Robert awoke, and was surprisingly chirpy, he said he felt at peace. During that night, God had spoken to him and told him that whatever was to follow, he would survive. Please don't misread this, God did not say that Robert would be healed and restored, although this was obviously what we would both have prayed for. No, instead He simply told Robert that he would survive.

Now, I don't know if you believe in God or not, or even believe that God spoke to Robert, but what matters is that we do believe, and we are hanging on to that word in the knowledge that our God has come good for us before, and He can do it again. This word from God, turned out to be a pivotal moment in our journey. He made Robert a promise, so that's what we call it, 'The Promise'.

Going back to the diagnosis, neither of us had heard of an Acoustic Neuroma before, let alone the treatment involved, and as our GP had said, he also had no experience, so we were left in the dark whilst we waited for the appointment to some through. Unsurprisingly, quite soon Google became our best friend. I know that we shouldn't have gone online, but there was nowhere else to turn to.

We soon found out that this type of tumour was known as a benign tumour, or in other words, did not contain any cancerous cells. This was great news to us, and in our naivety, we thought that this put us in a much better position treatment and prognosis wise, but this is not the case.

They don't call tumours benign any more, and this, we found out, is because the word benign was always mistaken as being a less troublesome type of tumour. In actual fact, they now call non-cancerous tumours, Grade 1 tumours, then Grade 2 and up to Grade 4 being the nastiest cancerous tumours you can get. We also discovered that Professor Cruickshank was the foremost specialist expert in the field of brain tumours not only in Birmingham, but the whole of the UK and across the world. I quickly put Professor Cruickshank on my 'wish list' as the preferred Consultant for Robert, as of course, only the best would do for my beloved Robert, so we added this to our prayer list. Nobody else would do now.

Then, we found out that the state of the art Cyberknife machine was the best option for treating these types of tumours. These machines were extremely expensive and there are only five in the UK, three of which are privately owned and located in the London area, and the other two are located, one in Manchester and the other in Birmingham at the brand-new Queen Elizabeth Hospital.

Because Robert's type of tumour lied deep within his head, they probably wouldn't be able to simply cut it out. Imagine trying to core an apple without damaging any of the apple's flesh, and then you can see how complicated any surgical procedure would be.

Now we had another thing to put on out wish list and prayer list, the Cyberknife machine. Once again, we knew what we needed and prayed accordingly.

The worst thing of all of this was the waiting.

Waiting for the appointment to see the Consultant.

In the meantime, Robert's vertigo was getting worse, he was continually falling down, feeling dizzy and the fatigue soon started to set in.

During this time, Robert's other symptoms became increasingly worse. The pains in his head were getting unbearable and the feeling that his face was being electrocuted was also increasing. There were many times when we had to call an ambulance as I feared that Robert was having a stroke. We had been told that stokes or seizures were very common with brain tumour patients and we should expect these as part of the norm. Lots of time was spent in A&E at the local hospital waiting for the all clear to be given, the problem was that there was never a neurologist on call when we were there. The paramedics were great, and gave me some valuable training on how to visually recognise a potential stroke, which I put into practice many times. A skill everyone should have, but hopefully never use.

So, we waited, living every day as best we can, standing on God's promise that Robert would survive this illness.

'Call upon Me and come and pray to Me,
And I will listen to you. You will seek Me and find Me
When you search for Me with all your heart'.
Jeremiah 29:12-13

Acoustic Neuroma

What on earth is an Acoustic Neuroma? That's exactly what I said when we heard that this what was growing inside Robert's head.

Having done our research we found that this is a low grade (non-cancerous) type of tumour that grows right inside the brain in a little cavity the other side of the inner ear.

I can hear you saying that, this is great news it's non-cancerous. Well, OK, it isn't made up of cancer cells, but that doesn't mean to say that it's not dangerous. The thing with brain tumours, they are simply not like any other bodily tumour. They are inside your skull, lurking either on the surface or lying deep within the brain. The very fact that they are inside your head, regardless of whether they are a cancer or not, means that they are trouble.

So, let's get the 'at least it's not cancerous', thing out of the way. It makes absolutely no difference. A brain tumour is a brain tumour whichever way you look at it, and because of the structure and complexity of the brain with all the nerves contained therein, anything that is growing in there that shouldn't be there needs to be dealt with.

Robert's tumour is located the other side of the inner ear on his left hand side, slightly leaning towards the Pons, which is another name for the uppermost part of the brain stem.

As soon as you hear the words 'brain stem', you know it's serious. If the tumour grows towards the brain stem and eventually crushes it even a tiny bit, and bear in mind just how minute these nerves can be, then it could be catastrophic. Paralysis, loss of functions, or worse should it be allowed to grow unchecked.

The initial symptoms are usually, hearing problems, perhaps some deafness, vertigo, dizziness, the feeling of a very 'full' or blocked ear, facial pain, tingling sensations across that side of the face from the top of your forehead to your chin, funny metallic taste in the mouth, and in some cases a dropped side of the face, a bit like Bell's Palsy. In addition, the patient could also have difficulty walking because of the balance issues, so stumbles around a lot appearing as if they have had a glass or two.

Although these are particularly slow growing tumours, they have such a small space to occupy and are surrounded by the trigeminal nerve, very close to the brain stem at the top of your spinal cord. Because of the location of the tumour and the surrounding nerve structures, they can cause a lot of nasty symptoms and more importantly a lot of damage should they be allowed to grow, even at a slow rate.

If you imagine how small a nerve is, you can see how even a small amount of growth can cause a major issue. Facial paralysis is not uncommon, as are sight issues should the tumour press or damage the optic nerve or part of the facial nerves feeding from the trigeminal nerve.

We have met some lovely people who have lived with this type of tumour for many years, having had numerous surgeries and treatments to keep them going. Then we have met others who have not been so fortunate, and have not made it.

It must feel like having a ticking time bomb in your head. I can't imagine what that feels like, or what effect this has on your mental health, just knowing that you could experience a stroke, seizure or worse at any time.

I haven't even mentioned the pain. The pain from the crushing of the trigeminal nerve is known as the 'suicide pain' as it is so intense and unbearable. Another aspect of this tumour, as with many other types of tumour, and other illnesses of course, is the fatigue. I often hear people say, "I know exactly what you mean, I am so tired as I haven't slept properly for ages."

This is not fatigue.

Fatigue, is when you have so little energy you can hardly move. If you have experienced this you will know how hard this can be.

Should you have the energy to get out of bed in the morning, it will have taken you an immense effort, and it's likely that this exertion alone, would have used up any spare energy you may have had to start with.

A friend explained this this very well with this analogy. Imagine you are given a pile of spoons first thing each morning. These spoons can be a mixture of tea spoons, pudding spoons and larger serving spoons. These are the only spoons you are going to be given today. Each spoon represents some of your energy.

When you wake up and start to get up, you may use one spoon to get out of bed and to the bathroom, another used up for getting dressed, and more for getting downstairs and making breakfast.

Pretty soon, as your day progresses, your spoons are being used up, and some days, depending on what you do, you may have used up all your spoons before lunch time, and some days, you may have just enough to see the day through.

The point is, that you only have so many spoons per day, and when they are gone, they are gone. This reflects your energy levels; once it is gone, there is no more until you have rested and got your strength back, and that may not be until tomorrow.

When Panic Sets In

When we initially saw our GP, we were told that Robert had to stop driving immediately, not because his type of tumour was the sort you had to notify the DVLA about, but just for his and everyone else's own safety. This in itself became a problem.

We had two cars and not knowing when Robert would be able to drive again while keeping up two monthly payments on the cars was simply not an option. So we decided to part exchange the two cars and buy one for us both. Sadly, this too created a problem as since the financial crash in 2008 our credit had not repaired itself and we were left in the unfortunate position of being unable to obtain finance for the replacement car. Thankfully, my wonderful parents came to the rescue with a loan so that we could at least have some transport during what was a very difficult time.

As you know, we are self-employed and had to re-invent our businesses after the recession. The work we are now involved in seems to have been pre-destined to fit our new circumstances, as we certainly have had to follow our own advice as far as money is concerned. It did seem like we were in just the right businesses and the shoe was well and truly on the other foot now!

Because of Robert's symptoms, it became extremely difficult for him to work full time. Even though our offices are only located a very short walk from our home, it was evident that he wasn't able to continue as normal. This became a huge burden, because as well as finding the means to pay our bills, including the mortgage on our home, we also had contractual obligations to our office running costs, which included one part-time member of staff.

Nobody tells you how to manage this. They just tell you that your husband has a primary brain tumour and then you are left to get on with it. Being self-employed, it's not simply a case of doing the work as it comes in, but you also have to be a marketing and sales expert to get the next pile of business in to replace that which you have just completed, and at the same time, keep on top of the office expenses, accounts, FCA Reporting, VAT Returns, etc.

As a wife and business partner, I found this very hard. On one hand, I tried to take the burden off Robert, so he felt that he didn't need to come to the office, and on the other hand, I needed him to step up to the mark and help me continue the businesses so that we could try and earn a buffer of funds in case we needed extended time out later on. I quickly realised that I had to become a superwoman. I guess it wasn't even a decision I came to, it just happened. I worked my socks off, trying to keep everything going at work and then coming home and doing it all again.

Money became a huge issue. As a professional debt advisor and counsellor, I knew what we had to do. We had to scale everything down to the bare bones. This was the first time I had actually had to follow my own advice. I was so grateful that I had this knowledge, and the skills to take a step back and review our finances and make necessary, if difficult, changes.

Even making significant cuts to our living expenses we found life becoming increasingly hard. I tried to step up my jewellery and crafts business by attending lots of craft fayres, country shows, and arranging workshops in an attempt to sell more to make ends meet, but as with all of these type of events, it can be hit and miss as to how you do on the day. I did manage to get a part time teaching job once a week at a local special school providing a craft session for some of the older children. It hardly paid anything, but it was great fun.

Our finances became a constant cause for concern and I spent most of my waking hours, and the non-sleeping ones, worrying about where the next piece of business would come from and how we would be able to afford the mortgage and major bills. We knew that God would provide for us, and trusted that this would be the case. You might think this is just us burying our heads in the sand, but it wasn't. It was much deeper than that. Amidst all the worry and angst, there came a peace, a peace that lifts you up, wraps its arms around you and tells you that everything will be OK, just believe and trust in Him.

I cannot stress enough how important prayer became. OK so I know that being Christians means that prayer is a biggie, but it's only when you are on your knees desperately crying out to God that the importance of prayer becomes a reality and not a routine. It would have been easy to blame God for our situation, and ask, "why us?", and I wouldn't blame anyone for asking this.

From our perspective, God was always there with us, and remains so. We know that God has a clear purpose for our lives, and who's to say that the whole brain tumour situation is not a vital part of these plans.

I have friends who have lost loved ones, husbands, children, taken away far too soon. They cannot understand why they have lost these precious souls too early. I am not saying that God takes people just for the sake of it, but maybe there is a greater and higher purpose that we just don't know about, and that their passing has been the catalyst to benefit many more people. Please don't get me wrong, and I don't mean to disrespect anyone else's grief, this is just my opinion.

Just think, if my own first marriage had resulted in a child, perhaps our relationship would never have broken down. I would never have met Robert, would never have worked in the field of money and debts, would never have been involved in cancer and brain tumour charities giving debt and end of life financial advice, and would never have been a supportive wife to Robert through this difficult time, and would certainly not be writing this book you are reading right now.

 I'm not saying that this is true for every case, but I am absolutely positive that every stage of my life to date has been carefully stage managed by God, and even when I let go of His hand and ignore Him, and do things my own way, He lets me carry on until I turn around, reach for His hand and re-join the path He has for me. This verse sums it all up for me...

"Never will I leave you; never will I forsake you."

Hebrews 13:15

The next thing we did may sound a bit morbid; we updated our Wills. Not because we thought we were facing death, but just in case.

Being told you have a brain tumour really focuses the mind. At the point of diagnosis, you have no idea what is to follow, and some people don't want to know. We decided whatever is presented to us, we will deal with. We knew it was going to be a rocky road but with God's grace we will walk, crawl or stumble over it together.

It's so important to have your affairs in order and it does give you a real sense of accomplishment in a funny kind of way. Making a Will is also a great way to leave something to a charity or organisation that needs funds for research and support. You can leave as little or as much as you like, it's up to you.

The next thing we did was to set up a Lasting Power of Attorney for Robert. I was noted as the Attorney. This would enable me to make any financial or health and welfare decisions should Robert lose mental capacity in the future. A decision we hope we never need to rely on, but if we do, then everything is in its place.

We also talked about our funeral wishes. This is something every couple should do. It's not morbid, it's kind of liberating to know exactly what your loved one wants, or doesn't want, and that they know your wishes too. There are so many hymns and songs we love and it's hard narrowing them down, but we both have an idea of what the other wants now and what type of service we would like. I expect we will probably change our minds many times before they are needed, but you never know what's around the corner.

I hope we don't need any of this before our old age, but having had these conversations, things were said that have brought us closer together, and will make our remaining time together all that much sweeter.

Now that these arrangements have been set in place we can concentrate on the important stuff, like treatment, recovery, and having some fun of course. What did become evident was that when you are hit with a life changing situation like this, everything changes. What may have seemed important a few weeks ago, was no longer even on our radar. There was a total shift in our priorities, which in its own way became part of our healing therapy. We no longer sweat the small stuff, we have much bigger mountains to climb now.

Live is for living, so go ahead and live it.

A Whole New World

We quickly became engrossed, or possibly even a little obsessed, with the world of brain tumours.

Isn't it funny when something new occupies your mind, it appears everywhere. All of a sudden there were people on television who were being diagnosed with brain tumours. People we knew on social media etc., were telling us of their relatives with brain tumours. Suddenly, we were surrounded!

Having spent endless hours researching this condition, and looking for information on what we might expect in the future, we discovered a whole new world had opened itself to us. A world we never even knew existed, and why would we? We had never known anyone with a brain tumour before, and it seemed like we had been whisked up by a tornado and plonked down right outside a big solid door with a sign on which read *'Brain Tumour's Enter Here'*.

It was a door we didn't want to open, but both knew we had no choice. It would have been lovely to have woken up one morning and found that everything that had happened so far had just been a really scary dream, and that life would continue as normal.

The door remained, still daunting, still very large, and now slightly ajar, we knew we had to go through it. We gingerly stepped over the threshold, and were wholly unprepared for what was on the other side.

Upon entering this new world, our first contact with anything brain tumour related was the discovery of a group called BANA (British Acoustic Neuroma Association). This is a UK based charity which specialises in our type of tumour, and coincidently, was holding a conference at the QE Hospital in Birmingham, so we went along to learn more.

Big mistake.

As we walked into the Lecture Theatre at the hospital, we were faced with a large number of fellow sufferers of all shapes and sizes. Some who had had this condition for many years, some newly diagnosed, and some who had lost loved ones to this disease.

The thing that shocked me to the core was the state of some of the patients. There were quite a few with 'fallen' faces, like they had Bells Palsy, or a stroke or something. Many couldn't walk without an aid or a companion, many who could walk unaided, stumbled and were unable to walk in a straight line. Nearly all were deaf, either profoundly or in part, and there were many speech impediments.

33

Talk about being thrown in the deep end.

Was this what was in store for Robert? I remember feeling a deep sense of despair as to what he could potentially end up like. Not for me, but for his own quality of life. I could sense that Robert felt exactly the same, and we sat through the lectures surrounded by a shroud of numbness and hardly hearing a word of what was being said. We held hands tightly to comfort each other without saying a word.

At one point, they offered people a tour of the Cyberknife treatment suite, and we jumped at the chance as our appointment was less than two weeks away, and it would be an ideal opportunity to see first-hand what it was like. Many other sufferers also wanted to come on the tour, and with many of them having walking difficulties, I ended up being a walking support having one patient on each arm. It must have looked a comical sight as we trundled down the corridors, bumping into walls etc., as they veered all over the place! Such a lovely bunch of people, all dealing with this illness in their own ways.

After that day, we decided not to attend any further gatherings with BANA as it was all a bit too painful and close to home.

Our next venture into Brain Tumour World was the first visit to our first Consultant. Mr Hartley was an oncologist based at the Queen Elizabeth Hospital in Birmingham. The appointment had come through and we saw him together. He explained that this tumour was low grade, and although not cancerous was a tricky little bugger to sort out. He decided that he would refer Robert to his colleague, Professor Garth Cruickshank. As soon as we heard this name we were overjoyed. This was the very professional we had prayed for.

This was the beginning of the answers to our prayers.

Professor Cruickshank, is one of the foremost specialists not only in the UK, but worldwide in his field. His proper title is Professor of Neurosciences and Neurosurgery. There is nothing this great man doesn't know about the brain. He is responsible for all neurosurgery at the Queen Elizabeth Hospital, along with the lecturing at Birmingham University's Medical School. He's one smart cookie.

We then waited for a further appointment to come through to see the Professor, it didn't take too long, and once again we were at the Q.E. Hospital, but this time was different. The Professor is a tall, lean, snowy haired man with a matching beard, just like Father Christmas. I think he must be related to Santa, as he has a lovely kind face and a charming nature. You know you've got the good guy, when the nurses all rush to his attention and nothing is too much trouble.

More scans were ordered and these would show the tumour in a lot more detail so that a treatment plan could be produced. Surgery was ruled out immediately, as the Professor said he wanted to avoid all surgery if there were other options available. In fact, he actually said that if it was him in this situation, the last thing he would have wanted was some brain surgeon inside his head!

It was then he mentioned Cyberknife, and yes, there we have it another answer to prayer.

"The LORD has heard my supplication,

The LORD receives my prayer".

Psalm 6:9

Cyberknife

It was the summer of 2015 when we were scheduled to have the Cyberknife treatment, and prior to this there were many appointments for further scans.

For the actual procedure, a mask has to be made to fit the patient. This mask is moulded on the face of the patient using a warmed plastic mesh surrounded on a solid frame. Whilst lying down, the patient is told to keep as still as possible whilst the warmed pliable mesh is placed over the entire face and pulled down towards the base of the bench creating a tight fit. It is in fact so tight a fit that the patient cannot move a muscle, even blink. The mould hardens very quickly, and this will be used in the actual treatment on the Cyberknife machine.

Before the day of treatment, Robert had to attend a day of scans which were taken using the mould so that the team could use the scan results to pinpoint the exact position of the tumour. It's size and shape were also recorded so that the correct co-ordinates could be put into the computers to generate a mapping sequence for the laser.

On the day of the appointment, Robert was told the procedure would take about 1-2 hours, and that he would be allowed home the same day as there would be no sedation or anaesthetic. We were told that this was because there could be a possibility of involuntary movements under medication, so it was up to Robert to lie completely still for the duration of the treatment.

Not relishing the thought of not being able to use the loo, and knowing he only has a 20-minute bladder, we decided not to allow Robert any liquids before the procedure, for everyone's sake. This sounded like it was a walk in the park. A lie down for 2 hours and then home.

The Cyberknife machine is an extremely complex piece of equipment. Imagine a large room, actually it's a lead lined bunker, with a very thin steel bench to lie on, and a very large robot arm with a pointy thing on the end, and there you have the Cyberknife machine. I guess it looks very much like the robots you see on TV that are used to spray paint cars in the workshop. The arms dart here and there until the job is done.

The machine costs around £2m, most of which was raised by supporters of the hospital, not the NHS or the government, and each treatment costs over £30,000, which is a serious amount of money in anyone's terms.

So, the day came, and we arrived at the hospital, along with my Dad for moral support. The Cyberknife machine was all set up with the latest set of scan data and at a prior meeting the technicians had drawn up the co-ordinates for the robot to do his work.

We had been told previously that you could bring in your own music to be played during the procedure, as you would be fully awake, so we had previously selected a gospel CD for Robert to concentrate on. So, Robert was taken into the suite and re-united with his tailor-made mask.

Whilst lying on the table the mask was fitted and screwed to the bench to avoid any possible movement. This is absolutely essential as any movement would be detected by the robot and the whole procedure would have to start again.

The nurses and technicians in the outside booth called up the pre-programmed routine and set the Cyberknife in motion. This particular program was designed to deliver 150 doses of radiation to the tumour from 150 different angles in the time allocated. It's done this way in order to avoid any damage to the surrounding tissue, because if they just did one big blast, there would be a significant amount of tissue (brain) damage to the area between the tumour and the outside of the skull, which is known as collateral damage.

Isn't it amazing what technology can do these days? It never ceases to amaze me. We later discovered that this machine's technology was originally developed for x-raying bridges in the military! As with many technological advancements they start off with military intent and then get re-developed and transferred to the public sectors.

Anyway, Dad and I sat in the waiting room and an hour or so passed, and having consumed several cups of tea, eventually, a nurse brought Robert out and walked him over to us. I couldn't believe he was able to walk, albeit supported, after all that radiation. We were both so relieved to see him, and as advised, we sat and had a hot drink and a little rest until Robert was able to be taken to the car.

I think the dose of radiation really affected Robert, as when we got home, he slept for England, woke up, and slept some more. We had been advised that Robert would need a couple of weeks at home resting after the procedure, but knowing Robert as we do, he was back at the office a couple of days later, albeit part time. Robert had been told that the tiredness could be a problem, which it was, and continues to be.

The purpose of the radiation was to try and kill off the cells in the tumour to stop it growing, or at least to considerably slow it down. What we didn't expect, was the immediate complete loss of hearing on the side of the tumour, his left side. This was a bit of a blow to say the least, but I guess a small price to pay in the overall scheme of things.

During the following weeks and months, there was an array of further scans, tests etc. These are required as we soon learned that the down side of Cyberknife is the swelling of the tumour before it dies. It transpires that the swelling can continue from the date of the procedure for up to three to five years, and then the swelling starts to recede and they can then see if the tumour has died or not.

The purpose of the scans is to try and spot when the size of the tumour recedes, which would indicate that the initial swelling is slowly being reversed. If there is no change in size, it could mean that either the tumour remains the same, or continues to grow.

During the initial three years after treatment it is virtually impossible to detect whether the tumour is growing or swelling as the scans are unable to determine the difference. The only way to see if this is swelling rather than growth is to wait and see if it recedes, and if it does then it was indeed swelling and if not, then it is growing.

We never expected it to be such a hit and miss affair, but that's where we are with the technology at the moment, and at least it's moving on at a quicker pace than say thirty years ago. Naively, we had thought that the Cyberknife was a one hit wonder, and would kill the tumour immediately, and we hadn't taken into account the swelling period that follows, and what that actually entails. We quickly learned that the swelling causes an increase in all previous symptoms, such as facial pain, numbness, metallic taste, electrical tingling etc., and this was not what we wanted to hear, or for Robert to experience.

Don't get me wrong, we were extremely grateful for being able to have the Cyberknife treatment as this option is not available to many brain tumour patients. However, the symptoms that the treatment caused, at least in Robert's case, have been significant, and we weren't prepared for that.

Brain Tumour Warriors

Having ventured into Brain Tumour World, we soon met some other brain tumour sufferers. By now Robert had joined some Facebook groups for sufferers, mainly via the Brain Tumour Charity and Brain Tumour Support. Both of these charities are only small but are dedicated to raising funds for research of brain tumours and the support of sufferers throughout the UK.

I guess once you are a brain tumour sufferer, meeting others in the same boat is inevitable. A bit like when you take up a new hobby or something, then all of a sudden you meet people with similar interests because of the new circles you move in.

Robert found a lot of comfort in his Facebook Groups and has met a lot of fellow sufferers online and in the flesh and been able to share stories and experiences. At the same time, he has learnt a lot about not only his condition but all other types of brain tumours too.

At first, I did feel a little left out. "Why was Robert seeking solace online?" I asked myself. I figured the answer was that he wasn't seeking solace, he just wanted to learn more about his condition, and in that closed group I suppose he could talk about things to his fellow sufferers that he perhaps couldn't talk to anyone else about.

Everyone has their own story, and we know that there are many different types of brain tumours. Some are low grade and slow growing, some are more aggressive and eventually do not respond to any treatment. Robert has told me of some of the stories of the people he has met online and some of these stories are truly heartbreaking, with many struggles and losses along the way.

There was a man called Clive, whose mother goes to our church. Clive was around the same age as Robert and also had a brain tumour. Unfortunately, his was a very aggressive type and the outcome was not going to be good. Robert visited Clive in hospital, and then later at the hospice he was transferred to. They became friends in the short time they knew each other and Clive became a Christian so at least we know we will see him again one day. Towards the end, Clive was unable to speak and was barely conscious, but just for a few moments during one of Robert's visits, he asked Robert to take care of his mother, Jean, and made Robert promise to go to his funeral. He then went to sleep for the last time.

This is why we have re-named them, Brain Tumour Warriors, of which my Robert is now one of them.

When you are a Brain Tumour Warrior, every day can be a struggle. Some days the fatigue is so bad, you can't get out of bed, even if you wanted to. Then, if you can muster up enough energy to get up, after a couple of hours, your spoons have all run out and there is nothing left in the tank, so off to bed you go again, only to start it all again the next day.

Then, there are the days, when you wake up as fresh as a daisy and just for that split second, you open your eyes and forget about the thing inside your head, but then within minutes the vertigo re-visits and we are back where we started again.

There are also days, when you just feel rotten, you feel like your face is being pulled off and whipped with barbed wire at the same time. You feel like you are having a stroke, so the paramedics are called, they perform the 'stroke test', and after a while you feel OK again, but it wasn't a stroke, it was just the brain tumour playing up again. Sometimes you are dragged off to hospital to the A&E department by the paramedics, only to lie on a bed for five hours before you are told there's nothing they can do for you and send you home.

Sometimes, they don't let you come home, and you are kept in, poked and prodded, and then sent home after a day or two having had more scans which are inconclusive.

You quickly get into the routine, asking, "How you are feeling today love?" whilst keeping one sneaky eye on his face without trying to draw attention to the fact that you are checking to see if his face has dropped. Your car, seems to automatically know the route to the hospital even without asking. Even when you are totally exhausted and driving from hospital at something past midnight, you somehow seem to get home OK.

No two days are ever the same, the symptoms seem to swap around, so you get some one day and a complete swap the next day. I cannot possibly imagine how frustrating this condition is to live with, and my heart goes out to Robert when I see him suffering on a particularly bad day, as I know he's doing his best to appear 'normal', when this in itself takes an enormous effort.

This is why they are called Brain Tumour Warriors.

It's when you have the bad days, you need the support, and I think the Facebook groups have been a lifeline to Robert, as they are to other BT Warriors across the UK. I know Robert will never meet all of his online friends, but they are an important part of his journey, wellbeing and recovery, and I thank them for their support.

Of course, there are some real characters online, and we have met some of them at a local BT Support Group in the Midlands. People like Kieran, who himself a BT Warrior has been suffering for at least a decade, having had multiple surgeries and treatments and despite having a very aggressive tumour manages to maintain a great sense of humour along with a talent for some very silly jokes. Kieran is now an ambassador for Brain Tumour Support and despite his own illness has been a shining light in raising awareness and fundraising for brain tumour research.

Then there's Marjorie, a lovely lady, who does actually remind me of Mrs Brown on TV. Marjorie lost her husband and soul mate not so long ago from a brain tumour. We know she misses him desperately, but she continues to support the Brain Tumour Charities and is a constant source of inspiration for fellow BT Warriors and their families.

Talking of families, you can't really not mention the families of the Brain Tumour Warriors. Like myself, there are wives, mothers, husbands, children, parents of BT sufferers. It's not all about the patient, we need to look after the families too. Quite often the spouses become the carers and this creates a massive shift in the family dynamics, but I will talk about this later on as I feel it deserves a chapter to itself.

There is one overriding theme when talking about Brain Tumour Warriors, and that is their bravery. Every single one I have met is a true champion. They never complain regardless of what surgeries or treatment they have had, or are yet to have, or how much pain and suffering they experience on a day to day basis. Every single one of them deserves a medal for just getting up and ready to face each day, knowing that only one thing is certain, and that's the uncertainty about their future.

The support groups for the patients and their families are essential and are a great benefit to anyone living with a brain tumour. Just by joining the support groups you will immediately gain a greater understanding of the condition, what to expect, how to cope and of course, make some great friends along the way.

Brain Tumour Warriors certainly have a great sense of humour and seem to take great delight in sharing 'brain tumour' jokes.

What did one brain tumour say to the other? You're getting on my nerve.

A man went to the doctor's. The doctor came in and said, "Well, I've got some good news and some bad news." The patient sighed, "Okay, give me the bad news first."
"The bad news is that you have an inoperable brain tumour."
The patient looked very grave, and asked, "And is the good news, anything to help me with the brain tumour?"
"The good news is our hospital has just been certified to do brain transplants and there has been an accident right out front, a young couple were killed and you can have whichever brain you like. The man's brain is £100,000.00 and the woman's brain is £30,000.00."
"I'm glad to hear there's something you can do to help me," the man replied, "But, out of curiosity, why is there such a big difference in the price of male and female brain?"
The doctor replied, "The female brain is used."

"That's the thing about brain surgeons, they get inside your head".

"When I woke up from my brain surgery, I just wanted to give that surgeon a piece of my mind".

"They told me there's nothing to worry about, it's all in my head".

Friends & Family

When Robert was first diagnosed, the first people we told were our families and close friends.

Our families are very important to us, and we all need support when faced with such life changing situations, especially as we just don't know what the future holds for us.

Families are funny things. Some are close, some are distant. There's a saying that you can choose your friends, but you can't choose your family. This is so true. Fortunately, my family were great, they quickly told us that whatever we needed they would be there for us, as they always have been. Dad has been marvellous in helping with hospital appointments, visiting whilst in hospital and general running around etc., Mum, as always has been a constant source of fruitcake, Sunday lunches and various other things, very practical is my mother.

My sister, Linda has been great too, as she's had her own struggles to deal with, yet she's still kept in touch and offered help when needed.

Sadly, we can't say the same for some of our friends. I can't quite put my finger on it, but we have simply lost touch. I had a special friend, a lady whom I considered a close friend, and we got together over lunch every month or so for a catch up. Our friendship seemed to dwindle and although I still attempted to make contact, messages were not returned, emails ignored. This all occurred around the time that Robert was diagnosed, and I have since learned from others, that some people just can't cope being around folk with such a condition. They simply don't know how to handle it.

I suppose I can relate to this, if I had a friend in a similar position, what would I say to them. I couldn't just say "Don't worry, it's going to be OK?" when I haven't a clue how things are going to turn out. Would I steer clear, giving them 'space' and time to come to terms with their illness? Would I rally round, and stick like glue so they knew they were loved and had our support?

It's hard, knowing what to do, and I guess nobody knows how they would react if their friend was facing this situation.

Looking back, it was exactly the same when I got divorced. My first husband left me for another woman but we parted amicably. Most of our friends were 'joint' friends, and we lost touch with almost all of them. It must have been hard for them to decide who they wanted to remain in contact with, like taking sides. Not really knowing what to do for the best, they did nothing, and severed all ties with both of us. Such a shame, as so many lovely friendships were lost unnecessarily.

When Robert was first diagnosed, we had lots of messages, along the lines of, "I'm here if you need me", "You know where we are if you need us", "If there's anything we can do give us a call".

I've done this myself, and now I've been on the receiving end I will never do it again. They are just platitudes, standard little sayings we churn out to satisfy our need to tick off the offer of help on our should-do-when-friends-are-in-trouble list.

From now on, I am going to be different, and I hope you will be too. I will keep in touch with my friends, even if it's a simple text, telling them you are thinking of them, or asking if they would like to meet up for a coffee. I will make a cake, cook a meal, buy flowers, offer to do laundry. It's often the little things that mean the most.

Don't get me wrong, our little circle of friends did rally round in the main, and we did come home to little surprises on our doorstep, some of which were anonymous and for these were and always will be extremely grateful.

Being a BT Warriors wife, I can also appreciate how hard it can be for the family. On one hand, they want to know every little detail about the condition, the treatment, the prognosis etc., and on the other hand, they don't want you to feel like you are being interrogated every time they see you. They just love you and want to know what's going on so they can help you and keep you in their prayers.

Of course, it does seem sometimes, like the Brain Tumour is the only topic of conversation I will ever have in my life ever again, so sometimes, it's nice to get out with the girls for some non-brain tumour fun.

Support? What Support?

Aside from the support of your family and friends, and of course the medical team looking after your warrior, you need support for lots of other things going on in your life.

We touched on financial support earlier and this is essential. Imagine if your warrior is the main earner, as mine is, and he has to give up work, as mine did.

How would you manage financially?

Not all of us have life savings we can all upon, or insurance we can claim on for loss of earnings, if only we did. Some of you may be in a better position if you are employed as at least you would be entitled to some form of sick pay I presume.

For those of us who are self-employed, unless you have taken out a policy for Accident, Sickness and Unemployment, (we had one but cancelled it during the 2008 recession in an attempt to cut our monthly expenses), you are stuck.

Even if you are still working, there may come a time, when you need to cut your hours, or even give up work to care for your loved one, and this then means the second income is gone.

Let me tell you exactly what support is out there for you.

None. Absolutely none.

Of course, there are benefits you might be able to apply for should your earnings fall below a certain level, but these are not enough to live on and certainly not enough to pay your mortgage or help run the car that takes you to hospital on a regular basis.

If your BT Warrior gets to the stage that they are unable to manage day to day living, such as dressing, eating, walking etc., then they may be eligible for certain benefits, but these are notoriously difficult to get and we personally know of many BT Warriors who have been declined but are clearly struggling to live on a daily basis.

The system is flawed, there is no doubt. We also know that the system is being abused, which has had a knock-on effect against those who really need to claim to be able to survive.

We had an interesting experience with the UK benefits system. We had been told by our MacMillan support nurse, that Robert should claim for PIP (Personal Independence Payment), which replaces the old Disability Living Allowance benefit. So, we filled out the forms ourselves, as we had nobody to help or advise us at the time. We were scored 8 points which was no good as you need a minimum of 12 points I recall to receive any form of payment.

We appealed, and the appeal was turned down. This was so unfair. The whole experience was so alien for us as we had never claimed for anything before.

Suddenly, we felt that this wasn't just about us anymore but we were representing a whole group of patients who were being side-lined by the benefits system. Having discussed this on social media we found that our story was by no means unusual so we decided to take direct action. We contacted our local BBC radio station and were invited to participate on a radio show. We told our story and the way we had been let down and how hard it is for other brain tumour patients who might not have the tenacity and determination we had to fight for our cause. Our coverage on the radio station highlighted exactly how some groups of patients are dealt with and how rigid and inflexible the benefits claim system is.

We continued to press for a fair hearing and asked for a medical assessment, and this was ignored. Determined not to let this go, we decided to take advantage of the tribunal process. We had been in contact with Headway charity, and the Brain Tumour Charity, who although were unable to offer any practical support, kept in touch with us along the way, as they would be able to learn from our experience and use this to help their patients in the future.

Our MacMillan advisor was due to attend the tribunal with us at the court in Birmingham, and we had invited a representative from Headway and Brain Tumour Charity to come along for moral support, although they would not be allowed to contribute in any way.

On the day of the tribunal we all arrived at court and waited for our MacMillan advisor to arrive. She didn't. We were told by the clerk that she had called to say she wouldn't be attending today! We had two choices, to re-arrange a future date, or to represent ourselves.

We decided to represent ourselves. A very brave move considering we had never done anything like this before. So we gathered ourselves up, said a quick prayer and entered the courtroom. The panel we were faced with was made up of a court official, someone from the Department of Work and Pensions, a medical professional and a social worker.

It didn't start well, as we questioned what medical experience the panel member had relating to brain tumours. Apparently this was irrelevant. Robert and I were then interviewed separately, or should I say, cross examined. Fortunately, all the documentary evidence had already been sent to the panel in advance, so the absence of the MacMillan representative was not a major issue.

Once the questioning was over, we were asked to wait outside as they would be making a decision there and then. Outside in the corridor we were joined by our charity companions, and they both said that they had never experienced anything like this before and were extremely grateful that they had come with us as this would be a useful reference should they be faced with similar situations in the future.

Expecting to wait for up to about two hours, we were recalled back into the room after only 15 minutes. Not knowing whether this was a good thing or not we entered with trepidation.

Before we got the chance to sit down, the court official handed us a retyped assessment form and we had been re-assessed and awarded 27 points in total. I couldn't contain myself. We were ecstatic. We had gone from 8 points to 27 and were told that this would be back dated. This was a major victory for us, it meant the difference between managing our finances or going under.

Once again, our God, had come good for us.

The whole experience has given us a real insight into dealing with the benefits system and we have since been able to help many people with applying for this benefit. If you have been allocated a CNS Nurse, then they should be aware of local organisations that can help you with whatever needs you may have. Although, again, this can be hit and miss, depending on resources available in your area.

Aside from the UK Benefit system, there are a few charities that offer support. The charity closest to my heart is the Help Harry, Help Others Charity. Not only because its founder, Georgie Moseley is a close personal friend and colleague, but because the charity has raised an extraordinary amount of money for research into cancer despite its very small size.

It all started with Harry Moseley, Georgie's son, who was diagnosed with a brain tumour at a young age and made bracelets to sell to raise money for research into cancer to help others in the same position as himself. This selfless act of kindness, formed the basis of the charity, and was continued by his mother Georgie after Harry's death at the age of 11. I never got to meet Harry as he had passed by the time I met Georgie, but I am sure he would have been enormously proud of his mother's achievements in carrying on the work he started.

It's still a small charity without any funding and opened its first Drop In Cancer Support Centre in May 2015. I am privileged to be able to offer our services as the go-to financial debt and money advisor for the centre, and also provide Crafty Carol's Craft Workshops each month. Since then we have given advice to many centre visitors and have been successful in obtaining some significant debt write offs for patients who have found themselves struggling financially because of their illness.

The Centre offers a wide range of services, including emotional support and counselling, holistic therapies and social activities along with providing advice on hair & wigs, lingerie for breast cancer patients, housing, benefit and financial advice etc. Even if they are unable to provide the expertise you need, then they will find it for you, or point you in the right direction.

There are also lots of social activities for patients and their families to join in with, from movie afternoons, crafty sessions, afternoon teas, and lots more. Most importantly it's a safe place where you can just turn up and sit quietly if you want to. You don't have to talk about anything, you can just sit and listen to others, or just take yourself away for some quiet time in the jigsaw corner.

Unfortunately, there are very few centres like this in the UK let alone in our own home area, and it's evident that many more are needed which has been proven by the number of individuals that attend this centre on a regular basis.

Since the opening of the centre, many broken people have come through the doors and have left having made new friends and received help and assistance for their individual needs. Without these centres, there would be absolutely no support outside of the medical profession whatsoever, and this would leave patients feeling isolated and without the much needed additional support which is essential to their overall wellbeing.

Another charity which has been instrumental in Robert's wellbeing is Brain Tumour Support. Again, this is a very small charity and they offer a range of support groups you can attend across the country. It's these support groups that allow patients to share experiences, vent their frustrations, gather useful information and make some new friends too.

The Brain Tumour Charity are another charity that raises funds for research into brain tumours and Robert and Matthew have been able to support them in the past by taking part in various events. The most recent of which was an indoor rowing marathon where you could allocate the distance you could manage and row away raising funds for brain tumour research.

There are many other charities out there and they all provide a much valued service to the brain tumour communities across the country and beyond. If you are able to support any of these charities either now or in the future, please help them as every penny you give will make a huge difference. The thing to remember is that if you need help, don't delay. Get out there and find some help. There are some contact details at the end of this book of organisations that may be able to help you, and if they can't then they will almost certainly know of someone who can.

Us

This is a tricky topic. How has the brain tumour affected the relationship between Robert and myself?

As you can imagine, there have been a wide range of emotions flying about since Robert's initial diagnosis, from complete shock and distress to hope and determination, along with any conceivable emotion in between.

Of course, our relationship has changed. As I mentioned earlier, there is a complete shift of your focus and things that might have taken over your thoughts previously are now pushed far down the list. Priorities are re-shuffled and things we wanted to do are placed on hold. Anything and everything medical now gets our full attention and is prioritised accordingly.

I am not going to lie, it's not been easy. As you can imagine, Robert has experienced both highs and lows. The lows are the hardest to cope with. As with many other illnesses, along comes depression. Unfortunately, it's all too common and is often forgotten by the medical professionals who are busy dealing with the main illness. Patients can then find themselves unable to cope, alone and anxious, and the more they worry about the illness, the worse it gets.

With an illness that affects the brain, there can be many changes to the person affected, such as mood swings, feelings of anger and resentment, along with a sense of loss for the life they once had.

Of course, the nearest and dearest often gets the brunt of it, and I was no exception. There are days when Robert gets to the point when he can't do this anymore and lashes out, and being the closest, I get the full force of it. It could be something totally unrelated to the illness that triggers it, such as me cooking chicken for dinner (oh, no not chicken again, has actually become a standing joke at home), which sparks off an outburst. It's never anything really serious, but it's the straw that broke the camel's back. Sometimes, he just needs some space to retreat into himself and come around, and there are times, when he needs to be told to pull himself together and look on the bright side. There is always a bright side no matter what.

Knowing that it's the condition causing these outbursts doesn't make it any easier. I know that it's a side effect of the brain tumour, but it can be very hard on both sides. There are times, when I have quietly retreated upstairs to have a little cry and feel sorry for myself, before coming back down and facing the world again. Luckily, I am not the sort of person that harbours anything, so all is forgotten pretty quickly and we move on.

Our work-life balance has also had a hammering. Before, we would always be looking at ways to enhance our businesses and looking for new clients to build up a strong and secure business for our future. Of course, we are still working on this, but now the emphasis is simply on making a living and not making a fortune. We know that God's hand is on our lives, and this includes our businesses, so He won't let us starve, and He will give us the strength and wisdom to keep the businesses going, for as long as that's His will of course.

I have always said, that time is the most precious gift we have been given, but none of us knows exactly how much of it we actually have. This is now truer to us than ever before. Time really is precious, especially when you know it can be taken away from you at any time. Of course, we already knew this, but now we live by it. Not one moment of any day is wasted, we are not 'busy fools', but are aware that every moment should be filled with purpose.

Being married, this of course, means 'us' time. Although we do work together, it's not the same, and I know that working together is not for everyone, and it can drive us nuts sometimes, being in such close proximity twenty four seven. Many of my friends say that they couldn't possibly spend so much time with their other halves. It's never been a problem for us, as we've both got very different skills we bring into the workplace and are both well aware of the other's strengths and utilise them accordingly. I'm a very organised person and can multi-task very easily, juggling lots of different things at the same time. However, I do need to schedule everything in the diary so I can prioritise and meet deadlines as they approach. I also love being creative, so my diary often resembles a work of art! I like to think of myself as an organised creative.

Robert, on the other hand is the complete opposite when it comes to work. He often forgets to put things in his diary and is very disorganised, but his skills for problem solving and finding solutions to some of the most complex situations leaves me in awe. He's an 'out of the box' thinker.

Even though we work together, we don't count this as 'us' time. Work is work, and home is home. I'm talking about making time for us as a couple. My favourite time of the day is at night, all cuddled up in bed, or snuggled on the sofa talking about the day, and just enjoying each other's company. We have made a deliberate attempt at scheduling in dates too. This often involves the cinema, a meal out or similar. It doesn't have to cost a fortune in a fancy restaurant, a bag of chips shared at the seaside is just as much fun.

Taking regular holidays and short breaks to recharge our batteries is also essential, so we have now started a holiday fund, where we are saving for some special holidays and treats. Before the brain tumour, we used to love travelling and have been all over the world, and still want to travel. However, having an unwelcome guest onboard causes a whole new set of problems. For example, travel insurance is now very difficult to get hold of, and if you can get it, it can be quite costly.

Secondly, flying is worry. Although we have been officially told that it is perfectly safe to fly long haul after 8 weeks post-surgery, it still doesn't feel like the right thing to do. What if the plane pressure causes a problem and the whole holiday is ruined for Robert? What if he becomes unwell overseas and is unable to fly home?

Thinking outside the box, we now have this covered. We've discovered cruises.

Yes, we had never thought of going on a cruise before, as the thought of being stuck on a ship for the duration of the holiday didn't seem like fun to us. How, wrong we were. I managed to save up enough funds for us to cross the Atlantic last year on the Queen Mary 2. The only transatlantic liner in the world, and it happens to be the best ship in the fleet too.

My word, what a magical experience that was. It was an October crossing and we experienced the best and worst of possible sea days. The funny thing was that whilst the ship was pitching and rolling in a force nine gale, Robert was walking around completely oblivious as this was how he walks anyway!

So, we now have a new mode of holidaying and having already cut back on our living expenses considerably, we have retained this frugal living style to fund our new-found extravagance. There is so much do to on board that the time quickly went by and a great time was had by all.

Robert and I have also started a new hobby together; we've taken on an allotment. We had a meagre attempt at growing vegetables some years ago, but this was never very successful. We discovered some allotment plots very close to where we live, hidden away behind some houses and were somehow talked into taking on two plots which were completely overgrown and had been abandoned for quite a few years.

This is now our second year, and thanks to lots of help and donkey work by some willing volunteers, we now have two fabulous plots containing over twenty raised vegetable beds, a greenhouse, a herb garden, a tiny orchard, a working compost corner, and of course the essential BBQ area.

I know a lot of our friends and family thought we were mad taking on extra responsibility with Robert's condition, but in a funny kind of way it's been magical. The work has been hard, and we have struggled at times doing all the hard labour to get the ground ready for planting.

There is something wonderful being outside working the land to produce your own food. We have created our very own garden of Eden and it's beautiful. Being close to nature feels very spiritual, and in many ways closer to God. After all, He did create the earth and everything in it, even the slugs and snails that try to destroy our lettuces. Of course, Robert can't really do too much up there as the fatigue takes over on a regular basis, but we operate on a little work, then a little rest, type, of routine, and that gets things done, albeit a little slower than everyone else, but we get there in the end.

I can honestly say that we have both benefited by having the allotment, as it's something we can do together without talking about work, the illness, the bills, the housework, and everything else that pre-occupies every waking hour. We love our little oasis, and would recommend this to anyone in a similar situation. The sad thing is that I know one day we will have to give it up as it will probably be a little too much to manage, but for the time being we are enjoying our home grown hobby. .

One thing that has changed dramatically between us is the dynamics of our relationship. I guess we were never the typical married couple, as we are both strong personalities. We've never really argued, and although both of us have strong opinions on absolutely everything, we often agree-to-disagree rather than have one of us try to be the top dog on the current issue of debate.

We have learned to identify more keenly when the other needs support, and offer that support right away. Of course, with Robert being the patient, his needs will always take priority, and I'm fine with that. However, there are days when I may need to take time out and switch off for a few hours to recharge my batteries. It's important that we, as wives, carers, etc., remember that we too need to take care of ourselves otherwise we will burn out and be of no use to anyone.

Everyone knows that the key to a good relationship is communication, and that's certainly true with us. There is absolutely no point in bottling things up, or keeping your feelings under wraps to protect the other. We've agreed to share, whatever we are feeling, and that means, when we are feeling like we can't quite cope today, maybe if we are needing a spot of alone time, or just in need of a cuddle. Having spoken for hours about what the future holds and how we would deal with things if the situation worsened, we said everything that needs to be said, so all that remains for now, is just get on with it.

The other thing we all need is a great sense of humour, and despite everything this has remained strong in both of us. There is nothing better than having a good belly laugh at the silliest of things to get you back on track. You see, life is now all about making memories and taking care of each other. Who knows how long any of us have left on this planet. When we are old and grey and too frail to do the stuff we like doing now, at least we will have some fabulous memories to look back upon. Forget the business goals and ambitions; yes, I know these are important as we still have to live, but they are not the be all and end all.

Every day we give thanks for what we have, regardless of what we have gone through, or what is yes to come. We are truly grateful for who we are, who we have become and for the gifts of those around us.

Overall, it feels like we have become much closer to each other, and now have a deeper love and understanding as to what the other is going through, and of course the trials that others face too, which, can only be a positive.

I think we have both developed a new empathy to anyone in a similar situation, and can honestly say that although our journeys may be different, we know some of the steps you may have taken.

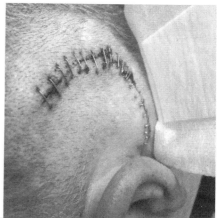

1. Robert with son Matthew – peas in a pod !
2. The scar after brain surgery, 23 staples.
3. Robert with Professor Cruickshank – the loveliest neurosurgeon you could ever meet.
4. Robert recovering in hospital after the operation.

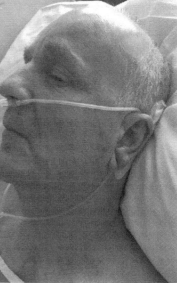

Team Matt & Rob raising money for The Brain Tumour Charity

Life getting back to some sort of normal. Robert back at the allotment and having a go in the kitchen.

Matt, Dannika and baby Everley who arrived in December 2016 and gives us both great joy.

Mum and Dad, who are always there for us, usually with homemade fruit cake, tea and some much needed DIY expertise.

My sister Linda, with her daughters Lucy and Bethany.

Not exactly Posh and Becks, more like Baldy and Specs.

Robert's looking much better here, and we will always be grateful to Professor Cruickshank and the team at the Queen Elizabeth Hospital as well as all our friends, family and everyone who has held us up in prayer and continues to do so.

The New Normal

One thing that we wished for at the very beginning was that one day things would get back to normal. However, we now know that this is never going to happen.

What is normal anyway?

Before the BT diagnosis, our normal was probably like many other people's normal. We worked hard, we looked at developing our businesses, we went to church, we socialised with our family and friends, had a few holidays, and generally had a 'normal' life of the usual ups and downs.

Working at the Birmingham Drop In Cancer Centre, I meet cancer patients who regularly want their lives to 'get back to normal', but the hard faced reality is that it's never going to happen.

This is because their 'old normal' life has gone. You can't get away from the fact that their cancer will have changed their lives. Just like these patients, our lives have changed considerably.

For starters, Robert used to love going to the gym. He loved doing back to back spin classes (yes really), rowing, some weight training, yoga and running. He also joined the mountain walkers group and the cycling group at Church and often disappeared at weekends going off cycling or hill walking with the men for exercise and fellowship. Unfortunately, the vertigo and dizziness has put paid to all that. Robert's balance has been completely destroyed, and he can no longer go out cycling or hill walking.

His gym routine has also had to change, and for a long time had to be abandoned. With careful planning, he can now go back to the gym once in a while and does enjoy yoga, except for the getting up and down from the floor part, and also the occasional spin class. The gym and yoga instructors are all aware of his condition and have been extremely helpful in setting up routines he can manage and do keep an eye on him just in case he becomes unwell.

The deafness is also a new thing Robert has had to come to terms with. Not simply losing all hearing on his left-hand side, but in doing so, has also lost all sense of noise direction. For example, he can no longer identify where noises are coming from and often turns around to face someone speaking only to find they were standing right next to him!

He's been fitted with a Bluetooth hearing system, which has made a difference. The device located in his left ear is a microphone which sends the sound waves via Bluetooth to the device in his right ear, and this then transfers it through the right ear canal and onwards to the audio nerves. It all sounds very technical, but the most important thing is that it does seem to work most of the time. The main problem we now have with the hearing is that although the system works great in most situations, it's not very good in public places where there are several layers of noise to contend with. Going to parties, noisy restaurants with background music etc is no fun anymore, so we pick and choose when and where we go with more care these days.

One thing that has helped is a sound bar. Having looked around for ages as to how we could improve the sound on the TV we saw a sound bar advertised. As soon as it was installed it made a massive difference. So now we don't need our TV volume set to stun any longer!

Working has also been a great challenge, as Robert experiences lapses in concentration, loses his train of thought mid-sentence and sometimes just can't articulate what he is trying to say.

Working hours and patterns have had to change to accommodate this, there are days when you can hardly tell Robert has a brain tumour, and then there are all the other days when he can't think straight, gets confused, loses things and just can't cope through the pain and fatigue. These are the days when he has to take time out and regroup ready for a new day tomorrow.

We have learned to be extremely flexible, diaries are constantly being updated and changed. Appointments re-scheduled, or I take them over instead or at the very least accompany Robert for support.

Life is now much more flexible and less rigid. We have taken stock, assessed our 'new normal' and adjusted accordingly. Life changes, people change and this is a very important part of our growth as human beings. It would be a very dull world indeed if we didn't experience changes, good and bad, and then learn from these life experiences and change course as required.

Because we appreciate that time is precious, we also schedule in lots of treats and time together. As previously mentioned, this can be in the form of date nights, time at the allotment or little short holidays or day trips.

We have always had faith, and faith is a big part of our lives. We've been fortunate in that our church has surrounded us in prayer and this has been a massive help to us. Just knowing that you are being thought about, that someone, somewhere, cares enough to get on their knees for you is a very humbling experience, and not just once, but regularly.

This in itself, changes you as a person, makes you more aware of not just your needs, but the needs of those around you. Being involved in the Brain Tumour World you meet lots of lovely people, all of which are going through their own journeys and we know that many of them won't make it to the finish line.

In the last two years, we have attended far too many funerals. Young, old, men, women and children. It's heart-breaking to hear some of the stories told by the families and loved ones left behind. So many people don't survive brain tumours. Even in the 21st century with the mammoth leaps in technology, we are still losing far too many warriors.

Having experienced the whole hospital routine, with appointments, scans, treatments, drug reviews, care plans, more scans, more follow up appointments, changes to treatment and care plans, we appreciate how exhausting this is and how it can have an effect on your state of mind, your mood, your relationships, in fact every part of your life. The effect of your illness or condition on your mental wellbeing is very poorly documented and at times, totally unsupported. The medical profession can offer counselling to help you but it does depend on where you live and the resources available in your area. We know that funding is stretched to breaking point. Depression and anxiety often go hand in hand with chronic illnesses and the effects of this are severely underestimated by the medical profession.

If you ever find yourself in this situation, please seek help as early as you can. Your mental health is key to your biological wellbeing and quite often if you are coping mentally, then the physical side often is more manageable.

We have both developed our coping radar and have a great deal of empathy and compassion to those suffering from this horrible condition. Whatever type of brain tumour you have, or any other cancer, illness or disability for that matter, all the treatment is more or less the same, and the effects of the whole process are the practically same for every patient.

At the end of the day, anyone experiencing a life changing illness, injury or disability goes through the whole 'I just want everything to get back to normal' thing, but the cold truth is that it won't. Every day is different, and we have no choice but to adjust accordingly. If we want to make the best of our lives, and our remaining time here on earth together, then we just have to get on with it the best we can. Our new normal, may not be the same as the old normal, and I expect in the future, we will have yet another version of normal to contend with and we will deal with that as and when it arrives.

But for now, we will take each day that is given to us.

Who am I?

The whole brain tumour journey has made me think about who I am as a person. Of course, I am a wife, daughter, sister, auntie, friend and more recently a nanny (yay!), but I am more than these labels.

I have been and always will be those things, but I am now much, much more.

I am now a carer, a minder, a physical support, an emotional support, the person who needs to remember absolutely everything, the personal shopper, the prayer warrior, the hospital appointment secretary, the taxi driver, the chef, the nurse, the housekeeper, the business woman, the accountant, the tax expert, the secretary, and bill payer, the banker, the (now) author, sometimes the emotional punch bag, the confidante and the one who holds him tight late at night when the pain is too much to bear.

The pressure is great, sometimes too great.

There's no getting away from the fact that your relationship does change and not always for the better. They say you 'always hurt the one's you love', and yes, that can be true. As a BT patient you have such a lot to contend with and you do lash out and say hurtful things to those around you, and it's hard being on the receiving end. Also with brain tumours, they often affect the person's behaviour and you soon notice subtle changes as things progress.

Mood swings are a biggie. It doesn't take much to tip the scales, could be something very minor like them not being able to find something or just sheer frustration of not being able to take the edge off the pain that particular day.

Every day can present a different challenge, but you just have to remember that sometimes it's the BT causing the bad mood or harsh word, and that underneath it all they do still love you even if they don't show it. There's a lot of biting your tongue and just getting on with things, or hiding away to have a cry for a while until things calm down again.

Sometimes I have felt alone, abandoned, isolated, forgotten, side-lined, desperate, overwhelmed and taken for granted. There have been times, just for a split second, that I have wanted to run away and never look back. There have also been times that I have been so tired that I want to go to sleep and never wake up.

On the other hand, I have also felt, deeply loved, worthy, blessed, appreciated and cherished. Thank God that I am now at a place where I feel valued and empowered.

One thing I have learned is that when you are caring for someone, no matter whom they are and how ill they may become, you have to look after yourself. If you crumble, you're really no good for anyone.

You may need to take time out and re-assess who you have now become. I don't think anyone realises exactly how a serious illness can affect the spouse or partner let alone the wider family. The emphasis is always on the patient and often the partner is ignored. I have found that the majority of people we come across always ask how Robert is and hardly ever ask how I am doing.

Most of the time it doesn't bother me, but there are occasions, when I do get a bit fed up of everyone asking how Robert is and not even considering that I may also be suffering. A kind word or a hug would have been nice.

Of course, there have been tears, and many of them. I have cried oceans, pleading for the healing of my husband at first, but when God promised Robert that he would survive, I redirected my prayers to the settling down of his symptoms and the strength to carry on through.

I do grieve for the life we could have had, and for the loss of the quality of life that Robert so desperately wants back, not for me, but because I can see how he misses the things he can no longer participate in. For example, Robert likes mountain walking and cycling, but because of his balance issues he's not being to be able to enjoy these activities any more.

There has also been a great sense of guilt. Not the sort of guilt when you've done something wrong, but the sort you feel when you think why couldn't this have happened to me to save Robert having to go through the pain and suffering he's had to endure. Of course, I realise it's totally irrational, but I guess that's what happens when you are in this situation, you don't exactly think clearly half of the time.

Since we had the diagnosis, life has changed for both of us. At the start it was difficult, but I have now settled into my new roles and developed as a person. My own health hasn't been great, with the scare of breast tumours causing a great worry, and then my own hearing loss; there have been a lot of ups and downs.

I also seem to be prone to stress illnesses such as impromptu viruses, colds and more frequently severe headaches. I know it sounds silly, but I really feel stupid when I am under the weather, after all, what on earth have I got to complain about, at least I haven't got an unwanted visitor on my head. I think that's a wife thing, not just a brain tumour's wife thing though. There have been many sacrifices but isn't that what true love is all about?

True love is when you would sacrifice your own life for your loved one. I admit, at the beginning I prayed, pleading with God to take away Robert's tumour and pop it into my head instead, because if someone had to have it, it may as well be me. I would rather have had to bear all of this than let him go through it. Not that I am any stronger or more resilient, I am definitely not that. Please don't think I am being negative, I'm just being honest.

Of course, we all know about the greatest sacrifice of all, when God gave His only Son as a living sacrifice for our sins, so that we can receive the gift of eternal life.

I have come to realise that there is so much positivity in what we have to go through in life. Even in our darkest times we can see a glimpse of light. I have been given the opportunity to use my personal experiences to help other people in similar situations, and for that I am extremely grateful.

Of course, there have been quite a few times when I have been consumed with grief. Grief is a strange emotion, to experience it you have most likely have had some sort of loss. I am one of the lucky ones I still have my husband, so what am I grieving for? I guess what I am trying to say, that there are many types of loss. Not only the loss of a loved one, which I can only imagine must be totally heart-breaking. In my case, I refer to a loss of my planned future, the loss of what might have been. Let me explain.

Robert and I married thinking that life would be OK, we would work hard, plan for the future, make a nice home, eventually retire and die happy. The sort of life most people are expecting, right?

Well, when anything life changing happens, whether it's the brain tumour, another illness or injury, or any other life changes. There's no getting away from the fact that things hardly ever go to plan.

It's the uncertainty that's hard, not only are your original plans out of the window, but that there aren't actually any plans to replace them with. It's almost too scary to form any replacement plans in case things change once more and you are left disappointed again.

We can't escape life's setbacks or even major changes, we have to adapt. We all need to put on the new hat and wear it with pride. I honestly believe that our lives are already mapped out for us by God's hand and that He knows what's coming and how we are going to react to, and deal with, these situations. He gives us the inner strength to carry on, but at the same time is aware that we need some time to adjust to these changes.

This is why I need to take time out sometimes. Don't get me wrong, I don't have any problem wearing all of these hats, but sometimes, just sometimes, I need to wear just the one hat.

Make sure you take time out for yourself, not in a selfish, self-indulgent type of way, but in a recuperative, restorative and rebuilding way. You absolutely must look after yourself, both physically and emotionally. Don't be afraid to seek out some professional support if you need it.

What really brought all of this home to me was one particular incident. In fact, it's the reason for this book.

One Sunday at church, at the end of the service, a woman came up to me and said, "Hello, I know who you are". I didn't really know the woman in question, but I am sure we have exchanged pleasantries in the past. Before I could respond, she continued, "Yes, you're, um, The Brain Tumours Wife aren't you?", she then immediately toddled off, before I could answer.

I could hardly believe what I heard, how rude, I thought.

This incident stopped me in my tracks. Is that really, what people know me as? Am I that insignificant that I no longer have my own identity?

I felt, hurt, as I bit my lip to hold back the tears, a flood that I knew would never stop if they ever got to the surface. How could someone be so unkind knowing what we were going through? Deep down, I guess, there wasn't supposed to be any malice intended, but nevertheless it did hurt. Not being one to hold a grudge, I reflected on this situation, and decided to use it as a positive, hence it's now the title of this book.

The Kindness of Strangers

One thing that has left us both absolutely stunned, is the kindness of strangers. Right from the very start of this epic journey we have seen some of the most wonderful acts of kindness.

The first was at a party we attended, it was still very early days, before we really knew of the forthcoming treatment etc., and we were both in deep shock, and didn't feel like going out to a party but we went anyway. I was chatting to some ladies, one of which was an ex-nurse, who goes to our church with her husband, and of course we got onto the subject of brain tumours. It wasn't her field, but we spoke about how the news had shaken us to our core. We shared that we didn't really know how we were going to cope and manage financially if Robert had to give up work for a prolonged period of time. I had met her on some occasions previously but not got to know here closely, she was a lovely lady and a great listener and gave me some much-needed words of comfort.

A few weeks later, an envelope arrived, from this lovely lady and her husband with a cheque as a gift of love from them both to help us out. This was a true miracle, as we were at a point where we were not sure if we could manage that month's mortgage payment. The timing was perfect. It was God's timing. We were so grateful that someone, not really a close friend of family would make the decision to help us out.

Some months on, we were at work, and someone, a friend from church, came to visit us. It was lovely to see him and we thought he had come to pray for Robert, which he had of course, but he also had another reason for the visit. He gave us an envelope from him and his wife, and yes, it was another cash gift to help us out. Again, the timing was perfect as we were at the mortgage payment date again. The cash gift was the figure we needed, at the time we needed it.

Another couple from our church, who were area leaders at the time, were Dave and Rachel Edwards. Dave came around to see us and had arranged for a team of volunteers to make us hot meals for a month. Every evening, a hot meal was delivered to our home, so that we didn't have to worry about shopping, planning meals and cooking etc. This was an enormous blessing what with all the hospital appointments at the time and all the rushing around here and there, it made such a difference. We even had help with Dave cutting the lawn too!

During that time, we were surrounded with blessings from all corners. People are so kind, we came home from hospital on many occasions to discover little packages had been left at our door, such as flowers, chocolates, magazines, lemon drizzle cake (yummy), letters and cards of support. The list was endless.

Out of the blue our church sent us a letter and a cheque that made all the difference. They kindly sent us enough funds to pay our mortgage for several months, which was indeed a very generous gift from their hardship fund. I cannot thank them enough for what they did, and again, the timing was spot on. We had hardly any money coming in as we were spending a lot of time at the hospital and therefore unable to source new business, and still had to keep up with all the usual household payments along with the costs of running the businesses.

One of the funniest gifts we received was an envelope popped through our letterbox to buy us a replacement polytunnel for the garden!

We had recently experienced some blustery storms at the time which had played havoc with our garden polytunnel. On one occasion, we had even spent the small hours of the morning outside in our dressing gowns trying to secure said polytunnel whilst the gale force winds tried to whisk it away. I can remember having to hang onto the inside bars with my arms upstretched, whilst Robert was trying to secure the base with concrete slabs, garden furniture and anything heavy enough to anchor the thing down. At one point, my feet left the ground and I was extremely worried that I would be taken away hanging onto the polytunnel frame in one great gust of wind, being transported over the chimney tops never to be seen again! I really didn't want to be party to the remake of Mary Poppins in our own back garden.

In actual fact, we did manage to secure the polytunnel, and managed to get back inside somewhat bedraggled and exhausted from our efforts, only to discover that our efforts were in vain as another storm a couple of days later lifted the polytunnel clear of our garden. We looked everywhere and found it a few days later all bent and torn in someone's back garden two streets away – complete with fairy lights!

I had posted the whole traumatic event on social media in case anyone locally had found it, and it was then that some anonymous benefactor left us an envelope with enough money to buy a replacement poly tunnel. This was a lovely thought and we are once again simply blown away (no pun intended), by their kindness. There are so many generous souls out there, and in a world full of the bad stuff, it's so lovely to discover these little unsung angels who pop into your life when needed. The Pastors of our church have been very supportive, and we know that each and every one of them continues to hold us up in prayer for as long as it's needed.

As our financial situation has improved, and by God's grace, continues to do so, we will of course, continue to 'pay it forward' and bless others as we have been blessed ourselves.

We thank God for these people who have taken the time to help us out and pray that they continue to be blessed as they have blessed us.

The Power of Prayer

Whether you believe or not, there is no getting away from the fact that prayer has had a massive impact on both of our lives. OK, so you may be asking, then if prayer is so wonderful, why hasn't Robert been healed yet.

The thing is that not everyone who is sick and gets prayed for gets healed.

There, I've said it. Shoot me now.

No, honestly, it's the truth.

There are many people who do receive healing and my mum is one of them. With only eight weeks to live she was miraculously healed of ovarian cancer that had metastasised to other parts of her body. She was prayed for regularly at our church until one day when her scans showed that the cancers had vanished, yes vanished. Compared to the original scans they were completely different. No sign of any cancer, and she lives to tell the tale, and keep us in cakes, thankfully.

So why doesn't everyone who has prayer get healed then?

I don't know simple answer. I do have a theory though.

Maybe, just maybe, there are blessings to come from their pain so if they were healed their destiny would never be fulfilled. Blessings perhaps for them, or maybe for those around them.

If you read about Job in the Bible, he was put through tremendous trials and never complained once. His friends and his family taunted him to give up on God, after all, what sort of God would allow this suffering? God knew that Job could deal with it. In fact, God chose Job especially for this purpose to show the devil, and the people, exactly how much Job could take and come through the other end without giving up.

Job lost everything, his home, his family, everything. He stayed true and faithful and although must have wondered what on earth was going on, he never gave up. Other people then saw Job as a man of great strength and inspiration, and that gave comfort to others going through their own difficulties.

Job was well rewarded by God for his loyalty and perseverance. Without Job we wouldn't have the saying about 'the patience of Job' now, would we?

So, it follows, that if some of us have to go through stuff, maybe there is a good reason for it. In our case, if we weren't on this particular journey, then we almost certainly wouldn't have been involved with the many organisations we now work with. We wouldn't have had the same empathy with our clients and we would certainly not have gained some of the most brave and special friends we could ever have wished for.

During this journey, Robert and I have received a lot of prayer. Many people across the world have contacted us to tell us that they are praying for Robert's full recovery. Now that would be great, but that's not what God said to Robert way back.

He said that Robert would survive, He never mentioned any healing.

This is key to the content of our prayers. We know that Robert will survive this, but that still leaves all the side effects and symptoms to pray for relief for. OK, so I know that Robert is in and out of hospital on a regular basis, with suspected strokes, seizures, severe pain, potential infections etc., but every obstacle we can overcome brings great joy to us and gratefulness that we are one more step closer to survival. Also, every different experience we see gives us strength and knowledge to help others starting out on this dreadful journey.

Through suffering can come great blessings, and that's what I am kind of trying to say here. Our lives are guided and supported by prayer, and we will stand firm for as long as we are able, by God's grace.

At the end of the day, we believe in a God that is compassionate and loving and created the earth and heavens and all there is in it. We are resolute in our faith and will stand firm knowing that one day we will meet him.

You may be thinking that we are totally nuts, and that's your opinion. If we are wrong, and there is no God, then that in itself leaves many unanswered questions. If there is no God, then at least we have tried to lead a pretty decent life, and at the end of the day we've not lost anything have we?

But what if we are right, and there is a God?

'I am convinced that nothing can ever separate us from God's love. Neither death nor life, neither angels nor demons, neither our fears for today nor our worries about tomorrow – not even the power of hell can separate us from God's love. No power in the sky above or in the earth below – indeed, nothing in all creation will ever be able to separate us from the love of God that is revealed in Christ Jesus our Lord '

Romans 8:8-39

The Operation

So, back to the medical situation. Last summer Robert's symptoms still seemed to be present, and were not showing any signs of abating. In fact, things were getting worse. The headaches, facial nerve pain, tingly sensations, fatigue, bouts of confusion and forgetfulness, lapses in concentration, dizziness and vertigo were all present in one way or another.

We had several visits to see Professor Cruickshank at the QE Hospital, and he finally decided that an operation needed to be performed. A date was fixed for August 2016, and although that was quite a few weeks away, the time flew and before we knew it, the date was upon us.

In the weeks before the operation date, I had deliberately made plans for the businesses to look after themselves. By working my socks off to get new clients and work in the pipeline I was able to amass a small pocket of funds to keep everything ticking over, as neither of us knew what state Robert would be in post op let alone when and if he would be able to return to work.

Looking back, this was the perfect thing to do, and I am glad I had the foresight to make these arrangements.

On the day of the operation, we arrived at the QE Hospital at the allotted time to book Robert in. We were both very apprehensive and did the only thing we could, and that was to give it all over to God, and place everything in God's hands, as after all, He's the only one who knew what was to follow.

Upon arriving at the ward, and getting Robert settled, we soon found out that the operation for the next day was still not 100% guaranteed. This was purely because before the operation, the staff had to have a bed secured in the high dependency unit for the recovery to take place after surgery. So, even though everything else was in place we wouldn't know if the operation was going to proceed right up until the last moment.

I didn't want to leave Robert in hospital that day, but I knew I had to. We said our goodbyes, and I left him lying there. I cried all the way home, and collapsed into bed, knowing that sleep wasn't really an option.

The operation planned for the following morning was called a micro vascular decompression. We had been told that the operation wasn't designed to actually remove any of the tumour as it was far too deep inside to get to. Apparently, it would have been like trying to get the core out of an apple without actually damaging any of the apple,

This operation was specifically to access the brain from behind the ear, through the skull, and to insert a sponge like implant to act as a barrier between the trigeminal nerve (the big one), and the tumour, so that any further nerve damage would be avoided in the future.

As with all brain surgeries (or craniotomies), it would be very dangerous and the operation would be around nine hours long, following by an extended spell in the high dependency unit afterwards.

On the day of the operation, I just couldn't settle, quite understandable really. The thought of them cutting away Robert's skull, and then messing around inside his head made me queasy and very anxious. What if he didn't wake up? What if they damaged his brain? What if he died on the table?

Far too many 'what ifs' for my liking.

I knew in my heart of hearts, God would take care of Robert, and his life was held in His hands. My mind went back to 'The Promise' *"You will survive this"*. This was the promise that God made to Robert on the very day he was diagnosed, so why on earth was I worrying?

Didn't I have enough faith? Yes, I had enough faith, but I challenge anyone not to worry when it's your husband on the table. We're only human after all.

I had estimated the time when Robert would have been transferred to the high dependency unit and arrived at the hospital. Having tried to call them for ages beforehand for an update, I did eventually get through and was told he was out of theatre, nothing else, that was all they could tell me.

I have absolutely no idea how I drove to the hospital that evening. My car must have driven on autopilot. At the hospital the lift took ages to come, but I was already too exhausted to run up four flights of stairs, so I waited patiently for the lift to arrive and emerged in the crowds of other visitors, and eventually got to the unit.

I was not prepared for what I saw. The high dependency unit is exactly what it says it is. Every patient is cared for on a one to one basis, they have their own computer station at the end of their bed with a nurse monitoring every reading, every beep, and readout being generated by all of the equipment attached to their patient.

The beds I passed all contained some extremely sick people, buzzers were going off, nurses scurrying around and, then at the end of the corridor I saw Robert, lying there. My heart seemed to sink, and float all at the same time. I was so happy to see him, but so shocked at how he looked.

He was wired up to every machine going, heart, lungs, bloods, drips, temperatures, pain relief, and oxygen. He looked dreadful. There were monitors everywhere and machines were beeping, pumping and doing just about everything to keep him alive. It was like something out of a TV medical drama. But he was alive, and that was the main thing. He had had the surgery and come out the other side, whatever happens next will never be as bad as the actual operation. The operation had taken six hours in total.

Professor Cruickshank visited Robert that evening and told us that the operation had been successful and in fact, he had actually managed to cut off a small section of the tumour that had grown a 'leg', which was something they hadn't expected to be able to do. This was great news and gave us both a real boost. I sat for ages, holding his hand, he was sort of awake, but not fully, kept drifting on and off again. To be expected, with that amount of anaesthetic inside you I guess. The relief to see that he was still with us was overwhelming and during that short initial visit, he improved slightly so we could talk, albeit briefly.

When I left later that evening, I got into the car, knowing that Robert was going to be OK. It would be a slow recovery, but we will get there. I pinned all my hope onto 'The Promise'.

Having slept a little better that night the next day was much better. My Dad was coming to the hospital today, so I picked him up and off we went for the afternoon visiting session. Upon our arrival at the high dependency unit, we were told that Robert was doing really well and they were moving him onto the neuro surgical ward to continue his recovery. This was great news, but I suspected that they actually needed the bed for someone else.

The new ward was less traumatic looking, patients were either in a small shared ward of their own side room. They brought Robert up to the ward where he would be sharing with three other patients. He was still delirious from the anaesthetic and kept insisting we had moved him to a different hospital entirely. The other neuro patients on the new ward were not much better, one telling Robert that he would be given a gun at 6pm to defend himself, one telling us all that we weren't in Birmingham, but were in fact, now in Australia, and the chap in the corner just kept asking for his dinner. It was a surreal experience, and Dad and I were sure we sitting in an asylum! This whole episode was hilarious and just goes to show how the drugs affect people.

On the ward, the life support machines were disconnected and only the drip, heart monitors and oxygen were left connected. This in itself, made Robert look better and the colour was coming back to his cheeks too. Dad and I stayed for as long as we were allowed, to sit with and talk to Robert, and every hour he seemed to be getting a little perkier.

Unfortunately, after we left, that night the patient in the next bed suffered a major heart attack and passed away. This was a great shock to the others in the side ward and really caused a great deal of upset. On the same night, Robert took a turn for the worse, it could well have been the shock of someone close by dying earlier. Robert's heart stopped and he had to be resuscitated during the night and was then moved to a side room so they could work on him without distressing the other patients on the ward.

This where he stayed for the next twelve days.

It quickly became my new routine, go to the office until about 1pm, jump in the car and head off to the hospital for the afternoon visits and then stay until 7pm close of visiting hours.

Everyday there was a new challenge, problems with the catheter, infections in the cannula in his hand, pain relief not working, and the worst of all was when they gave him medications he was clearly allergic too as outlined on his red wristband which caused untold problems. The care was good, but unfortunately it wasn't consistent. Some of the nurses were clearly very dedicated and cared about the patients, but others really didn't. I even had to shower Robert myself as there were no staff available to help him with his personal hygiene needs. The sooner I could get him home the better. This highlighted to me how stretched the NHS are and how close to breaking point our beloved health service really is.

The twelve days that Robert was in hospital were the longest twelve days of my life. Every day the same old routine, work, hospital, home, bed, repeat. I was getting near the point of total exhaustion. Even when I got into bed, I couldn't sleep, the thoughts racing around my head wouldn't go away.

I became an expert in list making. Lists of things that needed doing, lists of things to take up to the hospital, lists of people to phone, lists of shopping, and lists to remind me to make new lists!

It's so hard being away from the one you love, especially as you normally spend every day together. I missed him so much. The day Robert asked me to bring in his phone and charger was the day I knew he was starting to feel a little better. This gave Robert a real boost as he could now have contact with the outside world and we could speak and send messages whenever we wanted.

It seemed to take forever to get Robert well enough to come home. We had a few false starts which is very disappointing when you have a come home date in your mind. We knew they were thinking of discharging him when the nurse came along to remove the staples. It was during one of my visiting sessions so I was able to distract Robert with idle conversation whilst she pulled each and every one of them out of his head.

By this time, I was living in a complete daze. Juggling everything was becoming a nightmare, and I knew that when Robert came home, it wouldn't get any better for a while as he would then need my care during his recovery.

I was also getting countless messages via text, email, social media and voicemails asking me to call them and let them know how Robert was doing. I tried to answer them all, but I couldn't, so I apologise if you were one of those I couldn't get back to. Social Media was a Godsend, without it I simply couldn't have kept everyone up to date. I was able to post news about Roberts recovery every day without actually having to call everyone individually.

Thankfully, my family, and a few lovely friends visited Robert on occasion, which meant I could stay home and go later on in the evening. Pastor Peter Jenkins, Pastor Jonny Lee & Pastor Justyn Towler all visited and I know Robert really enjoyed seeing them as I am sure he must have got fed up of seeing my face every day.

The operation itself did seem to have gone well. Robert was left with 29 staples in his head which left quite an impressive scar. It was a neat little job which just goes to show how brilliant Professor Cruickshank is. We owe him so much.

On the day Robert was allowed to come home, everything was ready, I had freshly laundered linen on the bed, got a little bell in case he needed to call me upstairs, bottles of water in the fridge to keep him hydrated, and a fridge full of food to tempt him if he felt hungry.

We left hospital with a very large package of medication, including enough painkillers fit to knock out an elephant. In the days that followed, Robert slept quite a lot, read the paper, watched some TV, and generally took it easy whilst recovering.

The week after he was discharged he was back at church, to the amazement of everyone around us. His recovery was going very well, the scar was healing nicely and the pain was manageable.

I knew Robert was on the mend, when he started getting bored and wanting to come back to work. Obviously, there was no way he was coming back this soon, so I brought little titbits of work home for him to cast his eye over. Things that needed signing, draft letters for him to approve. Nothing major, and nothing I couldn't have done myself, but just enough to keep him in the loop.

It wasn't that long before Robert was back at the office. Walking was still a problem, so it's just as well our office is less than a five-minute walk from where we live and that he had me to hang on to. Of course, he only came back part time, but it was enough to keep him occupied and when he became tired, I walked him back home again.

106

Although technically the operation was a success it still stands that the tumour is still there and is still growing as far as they can tell. Despite the trauma of this very long operation Robert continued to recover and even now we take one day at a time. At the time of writing, we are now six months on from the operation and the scar has healed, and despite having a ridge where the piece of his skull doesn't sit flat he's doing OK. We are told, however, that this would most likely be the first of several operations over the coming years, so at least we now know what to expect.

You Look Well!

The funny thing about brain tumours is that like every hidden illness, you can't see them. We hear a lot about anxiety and depression along with many other conditions being described as hidden illnesses. This is so true. Just like any form of cancer or brain tumour, you can't see what's going on inside the body (or head).

Yet people still ask us all the time, "Oh are you better now? You look so well".

That's the thing about a brain tumour, it's inside your head and not on your face. If I had one penny for every time I remind people that Robert's brain tumour is INSIDE his head, that's why you can't see any evidence of it in his face, I would be a very wealthy woman indeed.

I don't know if it's me, but we also get a lot of people asking, are you better now then. I think they assume that because you've had one operation and you are walking around, speaking, and trying to live as normal a life as you can that everything is now 'fixed' and they can stop worrying/helping/praying etc. It's almost like they have a tick list of platitudes the roll out to anyone who is sick. "Are you better now?", "Oh, but you look so well...", etc.

Once they've ticked you off their list they can move on, but if you are planning on staying on their list they are not sure how to deal with it.

Maybe it's because as humans, we like everything in a box, and we can't deal with something that may never be fixed. Whatever the reason, it still drives me nuts. I have made a mental note to always try and ask the person how they are doing, and how they are coping, and also what the long-term prognosis will be so that we can direct our prayers accordingly.

I think as a society we all need to be made more aware of illnesses and conditions that are hidden, and that people do suffer without having to display symptoms. When you break your arm or leg or use a wheel chair or crutch it's easy to see that someone is dealing with a condition or injury, but when you are suffering from depression, cancers, mental illnesses and a whole other range of conditions, it's not always evident.

We are fortunate to have been allocated a blue badge for parking. In the UK this facility allows you to display the badge and utilise any disabled parking bays or in some cases park on double yellow lines. There have been several times, we have had comments or filthy looks from people when we get out of the car as if to say, well you two look OK, why on earth do you get preferential parking?

Through working with the Cancer Centre, I do often meet people for whom there is no hope. They have been given the terminal diagnosis and their DS1500 form from the hospital and left to get on with it. It's heart-breaking. What on earth do you say to someone who has just been given 3, 6 or 12 months left?

It's hard, it really is. I hope that from the road that life has taken us that we have a little more understanding of what they are facing, and what lies ahead and can offer some comfort and support when needed.

So next time you see someone you know who's been ill, please don't tell them how well they look, as they may just punch you on the nose!

The Odds are Against Us

Here are some sobering statistics:

There are more than 120 different types of brain tumour and these vary widely in their complexity, position, treatment and ongoing prognosis.

Brain tumours are the leading cause of cancer related death in adults aged under 40.

In children, the highest incidence of brain tumours is before the age of one, and then again between the ages of 2-12.

Less than 20% of brain tumour patients survive beyond five years of their diagnosis, whereas 86% of breast cancer and 51% of leukaemia patients survive beyond five years.

There are approximately 12,000 new brain tumour cases in the UK every year.

Brain tumour research represents just 1.37% of national spend on cancer.

Every day ten people will die from a brain tumour in the UK.

Every 2 hours in England someone is diagnosed with a brain tumour.

Did you know that Acoustic Neuromas (our brain tumour) constitute only 5% of all brain tumours?

At the current rate of spending it would take up to 100 years for developments in treating brain tumours to catch up with developments in other cancers and find a cure.

Brain tumours kill more people under the age of 75 than leukaemia and more women under the age of 35 than breast cancer

It is estimated that over 55,000 people in the UK are living with a brain tumour.

In the UK only 0.5% of Government spend on cancers goes towards brain tumours.

This is absolutely shocking, when so many children and adults are being affected. Funding is where it can all change. We can shift the scales in favour of brain tumour patients. For those of us who have loved ones with brain tumours, the odds really are against us. People who do survive brain tumours are often left with debilitating symptoms for the remainder of their lives. Often surviving does not mean cured.

Together we need to increase these odds.

If you can, please donate to a worthy charity. Even better, if you can volunteer, I can guarantee, your life will be so much richer for doing so. Please give what you can to your preferred Brain Tumour Charity.

Here are a few to choose from:-

Help Harry Help Others – www.hhho.org.uk

Brain's Trust – www.brainstrust.org.uk

The Brain Tumour Charity – www.thebraintumourcharity.org

Brain Tumour Research – www.braintumourresearch.org

Into The Unknown

None of us know what lies ahead for us, we have learned to live day by day. Along this road, we have met some lovely people from all walks of life, some of which are no longer with us. In Brain Tumour World, you get to go to a lot of funerals. This sadly, is just the way it is. One day it could be a bit closer to home, but we just don't know. That's why we need to stay positive, look on the bright side. Amongst the anguish and pain lies some truly memorable moments. Moments where you really see the heart of people and their compassion and where their actions show that there are some true angels out there.

We know from the research that it's very likely that Robert may die from his brain tumour, as it is perilously close to the brain stem. He could have a stroke, or an embolism, of goodness knows what. I guess it's the same for everyone as nobody knows when their time is up. We are the lucky ones, we have been given a unique opportunity to plan, take stock, and enjoy what time we have left, whether it's ten minutes, ten days, ten weeks, ten months, ten years or longer.

We also have faith.

Our Faith is strong in the knowledge that our time on earth is just the beginning and simply a stepping stone into eternity.

The Future

So, what have we got planned for the future?

Despite not having a clue about what's going to happen with Robert, we will take every day we are given and not waste a moment.

So we know our lives will never be the same again, and that some of our plans will never materialise, but hey, in a way the uncertainty is an adventure all of it's own. For every door we find closed, there are many more that are opened for us.

We have been so fortunate to been able to travel recently and although Robert can't really manage flights, we have discovered the joys of travelling by boat and have manages a couple of transatlantic voyages which have been fantastic.

Being by the sea is a great way to relax and regroup your thoughts and we now have a caravan by the seaside in Somerset, so when it all gets too much or Robert needs a change of scenery we simply jump in the car and head off to the caravan.   With the laptops and internet I can still keep on top of the businesses, which is great.

On a daily basis we meet so many people out there who are suffering and need help, and we want to use all our expertise and knowledge to help them. Whether it's with practical help and support, advice, or just listening we will do whatever we can.

After having gone through the whole brain tumour thing, I truly believe that we were given this unique opportunity to help families and individuals in similar circumstances. We now know exactly how hard it can be for both the patient, their spouse or partner, and the wider circle of family and friends. Whatever the outcome, they will all need a great deal of help and support from those close by and professionals.

As individuals and as a couple we know we have developed a much greater sense of compassion for those in need, whatever their situations, and many doors have been opened to us because of what we have gone through and continue to live through.

We have been given a unique opportunity to make a difference, and if that's God's purpose for us then that's the direction we will take.

It's now time for us to take action and make sure that anyone diagnosed with this terrible disease gets the help and support they need, when they need it.

I am already planning another book, possibly a sequel to this one, but I also have a book in the pipeline totally unrelated to brain tumours. This is going to be an interactive workbook to guide people who want to turn their hobby into a business.

We will also remain affiliated with a number of charities to provide much needed advice and support.

Acknowledgements

There are so many people I would like to thank and I am not sure where to start so here goes (in no particular order).

The Pastors, Leaders and congregation of Renewal Christian Centre. Thank you for all your practical help, support and prayers. www.renewalcc.com

Georgina Moseley, Kelly Nun and Jonathan Ford, and all the amazing staff and volunteer at Help Harry Help Others and The Birmingham Drop In Cancer Support Centre. You have all been amazing and have become great friends, your love, support and friendship know no bounds. There are too many individual to list here, but you all know who you are. Your friendship and strength are priceless. www.hhho.org.uk and www.bhamcsc.org.uk/

My special long-standing friends, Lynda Roy and Helen Lovell. You are what real friends are made of and I love you both dearly.

Mum, Dad, Linda, Lucy, Bethany. Thanks for everything, especially for the endless supply of fruit cake Mum, and all the running around you do for us, Dad, and Linda and the girls simply for caring.

Matthew, Dannika and Everley. It's been lovely welcoming Dannika into the family and of course our beautiful granddaughter Everley too. It is a joy to be part of your lovely little family.

To the Totally Fabulous, Jodee Peevor, who is a great friend, mentor and inspiration. (www.jodeepeevor.com) and also to Alison Smith and Elizabeth Gordon from our wonderful Monday Totes Fab Business Group for all your support.

Thanks to Alison Boyd, of Breastcare Solutions, who has given me lots of encouragement and makes me laugh.

Thank you, Carol Jackson, for keeping things going at the office when I am unable to.

Big thanks to Dave and Rachel Edwards of re:creates for their creative input into this book, couldn't have done this without you guys.

Thank you to Garry and Fay Steele for keeping it real with us.

And finally, to everyone in Facebook and Internet land who show their support to us online – thank you, we love you all.

"Now to Him who is able to keep you from stumbling and to make you stand in the presence of His glory blameless with great joy, to the only God our Saviour, through Jesus Christ our Lord, be glory, majesty, dominion and authority, before all time and now and forever. Amen".

Jude 24-25

Contact Details

If you would like more information or would like to submit a prayer request, please contact: carol@thebraintumourswife.com

Carol Shaw is available for public speaking events and can be contacted via email at carol@thebraintumourswife.com or via the website.

www.thebraintumourswife.com

Printed in Great Britain
by Amazon

82500566R00070